A LETTER TO HEAVEN

By Rakhi

'Whispers of a Daughter's Heart to Her
Father Beyond the Stars'

Dedication

To

Late Chitra Mani Naithani, my beloved father, whose love continues to echo in every heartbeat of mine.

You may no longer walk beside me, but your light guides me still in my dreams, in my words, and in the silence between them.

Acknowledgement

With a heart full of love and gratitude, I dedicate **"A Letter to Heaven"** to my beloved father, **Late Chitra Mani Naithani.** Your presence continues to guide me, your memories breathe life into every word of this poetry, and your love gives me the strength to carry on. This book is my humble tribute to the everlasting bond we share a bond that even time cannot erase.

A special thanks to my niece, Aadyaa, whose warmth and encouragement gave me the courage to pen down my feelings.

This collection is not just poetry it is my heart speaking to Heaven.

Prologue

Some stories are not meant to be told aloud.
They live in the quiet sighs between
memories, in the tears we wipe when no one
is watching, in the words we write hoping they
reach the sky.

"A Letter to Heaven" is a poetic journey
through those unspoken stories. It began not
as a book, but as a conversation between a
daughter and her father, separated not by
love, but by time and fate. These poems are
fragments of grief and healing, of memories
too tender to forget and emotions too strong
to silence.

They are for those who still look up at the
stars and whisper, "I miss you."

Preface

"A Letter to Heaven" is more than just a collection of words it is a journey through memory, loss and love. Each line echoes the voice of a daughter beyond the skies, hoping her whispers find her father.

This poetry was born in silence in the moments of grief. Losing my father, left a void no words could fill. These poems are my letters to him, the moments and dreams we built, the bond we still cherish.

This book is for anyone who has ever missed someone deeply. May these verses bring comfort, hope, and the soft reassurance that **love never truly leaves it only transforms.**

Oh, Dear God

Please deliver
this letter
"To My Dear Father."

When I close my eyes
You become the
"Brightest Star for
Me."

When I open my eyes
You become the
"Sunshine of My Life."

Oh, Dear God
Please deliver this letter
"To My Dear Father."

Thank you, to glow in my dreams
While I am asleep;
To say, "Sweet Dreams My Little Girl"
Thank you to be
"A Ray of Sunshine'
Holding my hand As I am
still your "Little Girl."

Oh, Dear God

Please deliver this letter
"To My Dear Father."

At night, When I'm asleep
Trying hard, never let you
Go up again.

And, When I open my eyes
Hoping, never let you
Leave my hand again.

Oh, Dear God,
Please deliver this letter
'To My Dear Father.'

Thank you, still singing
A "Lullaby" in my dreams.

Thank you, still holding my hand
When I am lonely in the "Crowd."

Oh, Dear God
Please deliver this letter
"To My Dear Father."

A life that was never before;
Was never supposed to be,
A life that was never dreamt;
Was inclined towards me.

Waiting for a "Miracle"
to happen
A rainbow in life
After so many adversities.

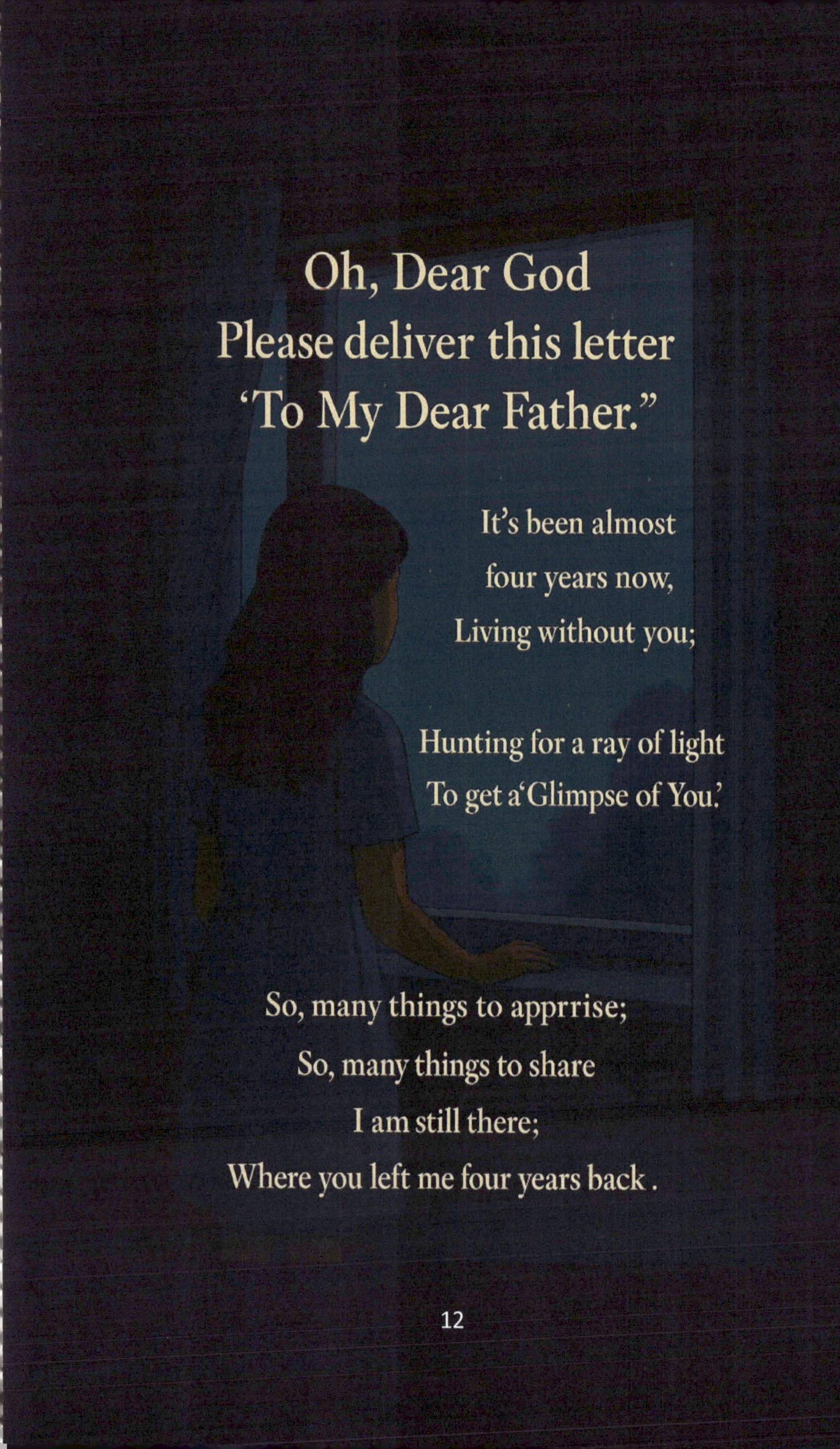

Oh, Dear God
Please deliver this letter
'To My Dear Father."

It's been almost
four years now,
Living without you;

Hunting for a ray of light
To get a 'Glimpse of You.'

So, many things to apprrise;
So, many things to share
I am still there;
Where you left me four years back .

Oh, Dear God

Please deliver this letter

"To My Dear Father."

I am standing at the end of the road

Trying to find the path

To move forward.

I am in a journey,

Where life has no meaning.

Surviving and Pondering

"Why do I have to exist?"

Oh, Dear God
Please deliver this letter
"To My Dear Father."

A twilight moment
When I am standing at et end of the road.

As the dawn breaks
I am striving to find the
goals to move forward.

Oh, Dear God

Please deliver this letter
"To My Dear Father."

Comprehending the connotations of existence
Whether, the life is filled with 'Colours'
Or, simply colourless.

Trying to clinge
The colour of hope
To bring back
happiness in life.

Oh, Dear God

Please deliver this letter
"To My Dear Father."

When I was born,
You hold me in your arms,
As the most valued gift from the god.
You were there, when I took my first step
You were still there, when I was trying to utter
It seems like, it, was just yesterday.

Oh, Dear God
Please deliver this letter
'To My Dear Father."

The childhood memories

Are flashing before my eyes.

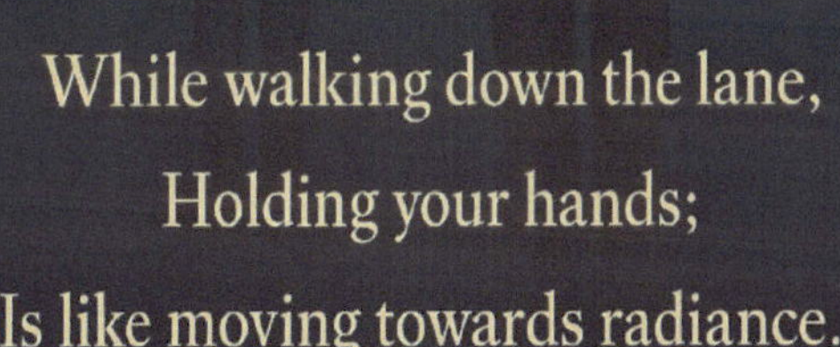

While walking down the lane,

Holding your hands;

Is like moving towards radiance.

Oh, Dear God

Please deliver this letter
"To My Dear Father."

Running down the memory lane
And, cherishing fond memories of childbood;
Seems like, you are around nurturing my dream.

Pouring happiness

in my dream

When I am in

a journey of

uncertainty.

Oh, Dear God
Please deliver this letter
"To My Dear Father."

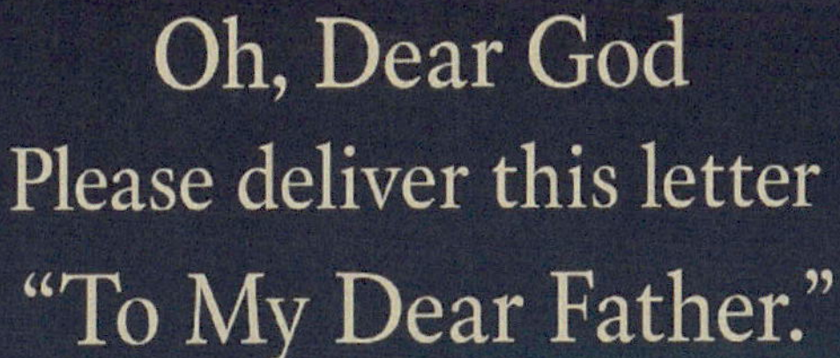

A feeling of your presence;
Pushing me towards
A new beginning.

Although, an illusion
I firmly believe to have
A new beginning.

Oh, Dear God

Please deliver this letter
"To My Dear Father."

The path of life
Similar, to "Change Of Seasons"
Has to go through an unexpected turns.

A "Life Journey"
Filled with both ups and downs
Just similar, to "A Roller-Coaster Ride.

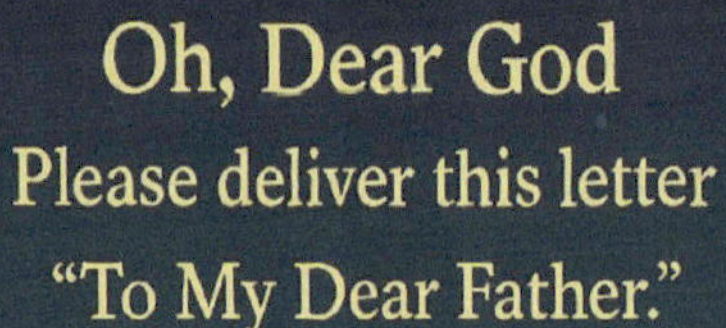

Oh, Dear God
Please deliver this letter
"To My Dear Father."

As the clouds disperse
I am on a self-discovery.

Going through my true-self
Similar, to "A Journey Of Life."

Oh, Dear God
Please deliver this letter
"To My Dear Father."

As, the time goes by
Perception for "A Journey
Of Life" is vivid;
Where we encounter
"Birth To Death.

The journey of life
Filled with learnings from the past;
Living the challenges of the present
For shaping the future.

THE END

About the Author

Rakhi is a writer of heart and memory whose words carry love, grief, and longing into poetic form. Writing this book became her healing process a bridge between worlds, between past and present, between a daughter and her father.

She finds solace in the stars, in silence, and in moments that whisper memories. This book is her offering to those who've loved deeply and lost quietly.

A Final Letter to My Father

Dear **Papa,**

Not a day goes by without your thoughts walking beside me. This book, each poem, each line carries you. I know you're there, beyond the skies, reading every word.

May my voice reach where my arms cannot. May this letter find its way to you, in heaven.

Forever your little girl,

Rakhi

For the Reader

If you've ever lost someone you loved, this letter is for you too. Grief speaks in silence. Love echoes through time. And in the quiet moments, may you find a piece of your own story here.

Connect with the Author

Thank you for taking the time to read **"A Letter to Heaven"**. If these words touched your heart, reminded you of someone, or simply made you feel seen I would love to hear from you.

You can connect with me through:

@ rakhi.poem@gmail.com

@ @chaimeintadka

If you'd like to share your own story, your letter to heaven, or a note about how this book resonated with you, feel free to reach out. Every message is a light that continues this journey beyond the final page.

With love,

Rakhi